A Hopeful Earth

Faith, Science, and the Message of Jesus

SALLY DYCK AND SARAH EHRMAN

LEADER GUIDE BY
SALLY D. SHARPE

ABINGDON PRESS
Nashville

A HOPEFUL EARTH
FAITH, SCIENCE, AND THE MESSAGE OF JESUS

LEADER GUIDE

This book is printed on acid-free paper.

ISBN 978-1-4267-1041-4

10 11 12 13 14 15 16 17 18—10 9 8 7 6 5 4 3 2 1
MANUFACTURED IN THE UNITED STATES OF AMERICA

FSC
Mixed Sources
Product group from well-managed forests, controlled sources and recycled wood or fiber

Cert no. SCS-COC-002464
www.fsc.org
©1996 Forest Stewardship Council

CONTENTS

How to Use This Leader Guide

A Hopeful Earth explores how to connect our Christian faith with our stewardship for God's creation. This leader guide is designed to walk groups through a study of the book, helping participants to link the teachings of Jesus to concerns regarding the care of the environment, resulting in an ethic of care and a challenge to our ways of thinking. Your group will be encouraged to move toward a more faithful response to God and to evaluate the views and practices of a culture that tends to worship power, technology, and domination over others and the earth.

As you gather weekly with your group—whether you meet in a home, church, or other gathering place—you will have the option of a 60-minute or 90-minute session:

60-Minute Session

Welcome / Opening Prayer **(5 mins.)**

Creation Crisis Question **(5 mins.)**

Scripture **(5 mins.)**

Connecting the Dots **(40 mins.)**

Continuing the Journey **(5 mins.)**

90-Minute Session

Welcome / Opening Prayer **(5 mins.)**

Creation Crisis Question **(5 mins.)**

Scripture **(5 mins.)**

Connecting the Dots **(45 mins.)**

Expanding Our Horizons **(15 mins.)**

Continuing the Journey **(5 mins.)**

Wonder and Worship **(10 mins.)**

In addition to prayer, Scripture, and group discussion, each format option also includes an activity or suggestion for application— one for individuals to complete on their own, and one for groups desiring an outside activity for a later time. The 90-minute option allows additional time for group discussion and includes two additional features: Expanding Our Horizons, which provides suggestions related to taking a closer look into a related topic, and Wonder and Worship, which is a closing worship idea. Of course, feel free to adapt these formats as you wish to meet the schedule and needs of your particular group.

As group leader, your role is more of facilitator than teacher. Your primary responsibility each week is to encourage participation and sharing by all group members. The more participants are willing to interact and share with one another, the more they will gain from the experience. Be willing to share first if necessary to get things going, but be careful not to monopolize the discussion, preventing others from sharing. Also be attentive to group members who may dominate discussion time, thanking them for their comments and inviting others to respond.

Be sure to respect group member's schedules by beginning and ending on time. If you see that a session is going to run long, make adjustments as necessary or get consensus from the group before exceeding the agreed upon ending time.

Prepare in advance for each session by reading the corresponding chapter in *A Hopeful Earth* and reviewing the session guide. Consider sharing leadership by inviting participants to take turns overseeing various aspects of the group session, such as leading prayer, directing Expanding Our Horizons, presenting Continuing the Journey, or leading Wonder and Worship.

Above all, pray for your group. Pray for group members by name, and pray for the group sessions themselves. Prayer is the most important preparation you will do.

It is our prayer that living as a good steward of God's creation will become as significant to your life of discipleship as reading Scripture or feeding the hungry. As you and your group think together about the connection between your faith and your stewardship of creation, may you sow good seeds so that you will grow in your appreciation and care of this beautiful and hospitable home we call earth.

Introductory Session
(optional)

Welcome / Opening Prayer (5 mins.)

God of all creation, you made this incredible world in which we live, and you have given us the responsibility of caring for it. Forgive us for our selfishness and self-centeredness, which have caused us to care more for ourselves than for your creation. We have become insatiable consumers, wanting what we want when we want it; and advances in technology have made us busier than ever before. We are constantly working, running from activity to activity, and connecting to our phones, computers, TVs, and iPods. We feel ultra efficient and connected, but we have become distracted from the one connection that is the most natural, life-giving, and renewing of all: our connection to your creation. Refocus us to the way that Jesus lived and taught. Help us to reconnect our faith to the environment and put our faith into action by making peace, protecting the planet, and helping to eradicate poverty. Give us "big picture" vision—vision that looks beyond the immediate moment to the long-term; vision that sees beyond our own needs to the needs of all individuals. Fill us with hope for our home, planet earth. Amen.

Creation Crisis Question (5 mins.)

Ask: What is the church (your local church and/or the church in general) doing about the environment?

Allow participants to offer brief responses.

Scripture (5 mins.)

> *The LORD God took the man and put him in the garden*
> *of Eden to till it and keep it. (Genesis 2:15)*

Read the Scripture aloud and pause briefly. Read the Scripture a second time, instructing participants to listen for a word or phrase that resonates in their spirit. Invite participants to spend a moment in silent meditation as they consider what God is saying to them through the Scripture.

Connecting the Dots (40–45 mins.)

Note: More material is provided than you will have time to cover in one session. In advance, select the leader cues and discussion questions you want to include, and put a checkmark beside them.

1 **The experiences we've had in nature, particularly in our youth, impact the connections we make between nature/science and faith.**

Leader Cue

Remind participants of the authors' stories of their childhood experiences in nature. Note that their experiences had a significant impact on their theological understandings of the environment.

Discussion Questions
- Did you enjoy or appreciate science when you were growing up? Why or why not? Tell your story about how you were or were not raised in nature—your nature story.
- Did you have questions related to the connections between science and faith? Where did you turn for answers? Who helped to answer your questions?
- What are your major questions and concerns related to nature/science and faith now?

2 Saving the environment should be a top priority of the church because the environment is God's creation.

Leader Cue

Read aloud the following, or communicate the points in your own words:

- The environmental crisis is actually a spiritual crisis.
- Because the environment is God's creation, Christians should lead the way in sustainability, stewardship, resource management, and species protection. Unfortunately, the church has not done a good job of articulating from a biblical viewpoint the connection between faith and the environment. As a result, caring for God's creation has become primarily a political issue.

Discussion Questions

- In what ways is the environmental crisis a spiritual crisis?
- Why do you think the environment has become more of a political issue than a spiritual issue? How might this be dangerous or harmful?
- Do you think the church should be a leader on environmental issues? Why or why not? What might this "look like"?
- Does the term "creation crisis" resonate differently with you than the term "environmental crisis"? Why or why not?

3 Environmental issues are controversial.

Leader Cue

Read aloud the following, or communicate the point in your own words:

- The church often neglects or stays out of environmental issues because they are so controversial. The controversy seems to revolve around how environmental issues impact people's pocketbooks and immediate conveniences. Greed and consumerism lie at the core of the matter.

Discussion Questions
- What is the church supposed to stand for and advocate? What are its stated values and mission?
- In your opinion, how has the church lived up to these values/this mission?
- Do you believe that the church needs to reassess its priorities? Why or why not?

4 Jesus' teachings align with the care of the environment.

Leader Cue

Read aloud the following, or communicate the point in your own words:

- Jesus' teachings reflect an ethic of care and challenge our ways of thinking in a culture where we tend to worship power, technology, and domination over others and the earth. Viewing Jesus as someone with an agrarian economic worldview helps us to understand his alternative, even countercultural, perspective on the military-industrial complex of his own day, as well as what and who he found to be important in God's economy of abundance and goodness.

Discussion Questions
- What does it mean to say that Jesus had an agrarian economic worldview? Based on the gospel stories, what and who did Jesus find to be important in God's economy of abundance and goodness?

- Why is it important to think deeply about who we are, why we're here on earth, and what our responsibility is to creation as followers of Jesus?
- Why do you think so many Christians today live their lives completely detached from environmental issues, continuing to practice habits that are destructive and harmful to the environment?

Expanding Our Horizons (15 mins. – 90-minute session only)

Most of us think of politics, not religion, when we think of the environment. The church has tended to neglect or stay out of environmental issues because they are so controversial. Plan to gather additional information related to the church's involvement—or lack of involvement—in a recent environmental concern (e.g., the oil spill in the Gulf). In advance of the session, assign one person to find out what various denominations or religious groups have said and done in response to the issue. Have another person research how politicians and political groups have responded. Invite the participants to briefly share their findings with the group, and compare and contrast their findings.

Continuing the Journey (5 mins.)

As Christians, we have a moral responsibility to care for the earth. The first step is to think deeply about who we are, why we're here on earth, and what our responsibility is to creation as followers of Jesus and to reflect deeply on how our mission as a church intersects with our call to care for God's creation.

A Commitment for Individuals: Prayerfully reflect on the following questions throughout the week:
- Does the size of the "carbon footprint" you are leaving—the way in which you interact with the earth and the environment—say anything about your religious commitment?
- If a stranger were to observe your "environmental lifestyle" habits for one week, would he or she be able to see any difference between you and someone without a religious commitment?

A Commitment for Groups: Plan a prayer service that focuses on our call to care for God's creation—as individuals and as the church. A prayer service is a great way to kick off this small-group study and/or a church-wide emphasis on *A Hopeful Earth*.

Wonder and Worship (10 mins. – 90-minute session only)

In advance of the session, find a short video clip of 3-4 minutes (e.g., see www.youtube.com) depicting the beauty and majesty of creation. Look for a clip that has peaceful background music, or plan to mute the sound and play your own background music.

Dim the lights and show the clip to the group while reading aloud the Creation story from Genesis 1:1-31. Then have a time of silent prayer and meditation, inviting participants to talk silently to God about what they hope to gain from this study in the coming weeks. Close by singing together the hymn "All Things Bright and Beautiful" or a contemporary praise song that celebrates God as creator.

1

SESSION ONE:
Our Three Temptations

Welcome / Opening Prayer (5 mins.)

God of all creation, your Son, Jesus, was no stranger to temptation. In the wilderness he faced three temptations, and these same temptations are our temptations, too. First, we are tempted to forget that we are the children of God and are called to live within the laws of nature. Rather than seeking a sustainable lifestyle, we look to science and technology to save us from the damage we have done to your creation. Second, we are tempted to believe that we are the pinnacle of creation and thereby have the right to do whatever we will with it. Once again this temptation beckons us to forget our identity and our calling, which is to be stewards of the earth. Third, we are tempted to use our relationship with you to our advantage—to expect you to exempt us from fulfilling our responsibility as caretakers of the earth. Believing that you will save us from ourselves, we consume rather than conserve; we destroy rather than defend. Help us to stand firm against each of these temptations so that we may fulfill our role as caretakers of the earth and all living things. Remind us daily of this holy calling, and equip us to faithfully follow in the way of Jesus. Amen.

Creation Crisis Question (5 mins.)

Ask: Do you believe that science and technology can save us from the negative impact of our careless and destructive living on planet earth? Why or why not?

Allow participants to offer brief responses.

Scripture (5 mins.)

> *Then God said, "Let us make humankind in our image, according to our likeness; and let them have dominion over the fish of the sea, and over the birds of the air, and over the cattle, and over all the wild animals of the earth, and over every creeping thing that creeps upon the earth." . . . God blessed them, and God said to them, "Be fruitful and multiply, and fill the earth and subdue it; and have dominion over the fish of the sea and over the birds of the air and over every living thing that moves upon the earth." (Genesis 1:26, 28)*

Read the Scripture aloud and pause briefly. Read the Scripture a second time, instructing participants to listen for a word or phrase that resonates in their spirit. Invite participants to spend a moment in silent meditation as they consider what God is saying to them through the Scripture.

Connecting the Dots (40–45 mins.)

Note: More material is provided than you will have time to cover in one session. In advance, select the leader cues and discussion questions you want to include, and put a checkmark beside them.

1 **We are tempted to trust in science and technology to save us from the effects of what we are doing to the environment.**

Leader Cue

Read aloud the following, or communicate the points in your own words.

- In light of the ways we are hurting the planet, sometimes we are tempted, as Jesus was, to defy the laws or rules of nature. Our temptation is to trust in science and technology to save us from the damage we are doing to God's creation. When we forget who we are—that we are made in God's image and are not God ourselves—we begin to trust in other means such as science and technology to heal and care for the earth and its peoples.
- We must remember that science and technology are the fruit of human endeavor and are tools that we have to make our lives better—or worse. Through science and technology we will find other sources of energy as we find ourselves at the end of the fossil fuel energy source. Science and technology can even help to solve some of the problems—and accidents—that occur when their respective disciplines fail us in other ways. Yet we cannot expect science and technology to solve the problems that we have created.
- We must be willing to make changes rather than to trust solely in science and technology to save us. We must recognize that the ways in which we live impact our lives on this planet both now and in the future, and we must live accordingly.
- We must make the teachings of Jesus our guide for how to live a more sustainable life.

Discussion Questions
- Why do you think we're often tempted to trust in science and technology to save us from the environmental problems we have created? What is the danger in this way of thinking?
- How can our faith help us to live a more sustainable life on planet earth? How might the teachings of Jesus, specifically, serve as our guide?
- On a scale of 1 to 10 (with 1 being low and 10 being high), how willing are you right now to make changes and "sacrifices" for the good of the earth?

2 Contrary to popular opinion, science is compatible with Christian faith.

Leader Cue

Read aloud the following, or communicate the points in your own words.

- Science and faith are not incompatible. Consider the origins of life.
- Both the theory of evolution and the story of Creation from Genesis 1 tell us not how things began but simply that they began. A careful review of Genesis 1 in terms of the order of creation reveals that it is not linear. In other words, what is created on one day doesn't necessary make sense in a logical way with what happens on another. The Genesis account answers questions not about science, but about relationship—God's relationship to humanity, to the creatures of the earth, and to the earth itself.
- The idea that science and faith are at odds with each other is a relatively recent phenomenon, spanning mostly the 20th century. In fact, because it is grounded in the concept that the universe was created by God, Christianity has actually encouraged scientific observation, exploration, and experimentation so that we may better understand God's creation.

Discussion Questions
- How are science and faith compatible in terms of the origins of life?
- What would you say are the most significant or meaningful questions answered by the Genesis story?
- Does it surprise you that the conflict between faith and science is a relatively new phenomenon? Why or why not?
- What historical and cultural events or changes have contributed to the disconnection between faith and science?

3 **We are tempted to make politics and economics our world-view instead of our faith.**

Leader Cue

Read aloud the following, or communicate the points in your own words.

- God created the universe and declared it good, but we have polluted it through our political and economic arrogance and pride. We have been tempted to believe we are the pinnacle of creation and thus have the right to do with it whatever we will. This temptation appeals to us when we forget our identity as God's stewards of the earth.
- Immediately upon creating all things and declaring them good, God handed creation over to humanity for management. Dominion essentially means "active management" or "mastery among"—as opposed to "mastery over."[1] It means to care for what has been entrusted to us.
- As caretakers of the earth, we are in an interdependent relationship with creation. "Shepherding" or caring for the land and its animals is an ancient and biblical example of an agrarian philosophy and lifestyle that supports this interdependent relationship. A farmer with an agrarian worldview will do only what is healthy and good for the land and its animals—not what will bring harm and destruction to the land, its animals, or the people who live on the land and are dependent upon its fruitfulness.
- If we are living in the image of God, we will be good stewards of the power and resources we have been given. We will recognize that having dominion means treating the earth and its creatures in such a way that the land is able to sustain life.

Discussion Questions
- Why can't we rely solely on the political and economic systems of our day to solve the problems related to the care of God's creation?

- How can we—as individuals and as the church—be a prophetic witness and influence in our day for the care of the earth?
- How would you describe what it means to be a good steward of the power and resources you have been given?
- If you were to take seriously the call to "treat the earth and its creatures in such a way that the land is able to sustain life," how would it affect your daily life? Think about how your decisions, your actions, and even your conversations might be different.

4 We are tempted to believe that God will save us from ourselves.

Leader Cue

Read aloud the following, or communicate the points in your own words.

- Many Christians believe that caring for God's creation is not a religious or spiritual matter. They see it as something that "tree-huggers and hippies" or creation-worshiping fanatics do—but not serious Christians.
- Many of us have succumbed to throwing ourselves off the highest pinnacle, expecting that God will save us, instead of facing the controversy that might arise if we were to point out the connection between our faith and a more sustainable lifestyle—for ourselves, the nation, and the world.
- The fear of raising controversial and potentially divisive matters of social holiness, such as caring for the creation, silences many people and keeps them from being the witnesses they need to be so that the principalities of business, politics, and science can do the right thing for the future of our planet.
- Renewing God's creation is part of the social holiness that John Wesley challenged us to live. He said that "you do not

become holy by keeping yourself pure and clean from the world but by plunging into ministry on behalf of the world's hurting ones." Too many of "the world's hurting ones" aren't visible and real to those who can make a difference. For many, a "social concern" has become a statistic or concept rather than a child of God. As disciples of Jesus Christ, we are called to a more "holy" way of living that allows others to live.

Discussion Questions
- How do you think the idea that God will save us from our exploitation of the earth's resources might affect an individual's level of concern and care for the earth?
- Why do you think many Christians believe that caring for God's creation is not a religious or spiritual matter?
- Do you believe the church can be "too involved" in social concerns? Why or why not? Does it change your viewpoint in any way to think of a social concern as "a child of God" rather than merely an issue?
- How is caring for the earth a part of discipleship?

Expanding Our Horizons (15 mins. – 90-minute session only)
John Wesley said that "the Gospel of Christ knows no religion but social, no holiness but social holiness." In advance of the session, assign someone to research Wesley's teachings on social holiness at a public or church library. Have them present their findings, and then discuss how renewing God's creation is part of the social holiness that Wesley challenged us to live.

Continuing the Journey (5 mins.)
In 2007, author and bishop Rueben Job resurrected and updated the language of the three simple rules that John Wesley taught the early Methodists:[2]

> Do no harm.
> Do good.
> Stay in love with God.[3]

He encourages and challenges us to attend to these simple rules as a guide for Christian living in our relationships with others and with God, based on the Great Commandment (to love God) and the second commandment (to love our neighbor as ourselves). In light of our Christian faith and God's creation, these rules also can give guidance for us and for our communities, churches, and nations in taking the next, best steps in living more sustainably.

A Commitment for Individuals:
- Look at the ways in your life that you unintentionally harm your community and the planet.
- What are steps you can take to change this trend in your own life? Write them down and identify one positive change you can begin to implement this week.
- Tell someone else in the group and ask him or her to hold you accountable.

A Commitment for Groups: Follow Wesley's advice and plunge into ministry on behalf of the world's hurting ones. Identify a group of people who have been negatively impacted by an environmental issue or crisis, and discuss ways you can reach out with love and support. Plan how you will vocalize and demonstrate your love and support together.

Wonder and Worship (10 mins. – 90-minute session only)
Lead the group in a prayer of repentance and commitment. For the first part of the prayer (repentance), instruct participants to respond in unison after each segment with the phrase, "Forgive us, Lord." For the second part of the prayer (commitment), instruct participants to respond in unison after each segment with the phrase, "Help us to be caretakers, Lord."

In advance, purchase an inexpensive, small plant (e.g., a flower or herb) for each participant (depending on the number in your group, you might buy a flat of flowers/herbs). After the prayer, hand out the plants as a reminder of the commitment they have made to be caretakers of creation.

Part 1: Repentance

Creator God, you have called us to be caretakers of the earth. You have given us the responsibility of overseeing the earth and its creatures in such a way that the land is able to sustain life. But our selfish lifestyles and arrogant ways have destroyed and depleted its resources.

Forgive us, Lord.

We have seen the ecological damage we have caused to the environment. We have experienced the effects of diminishing resources. And we have allowed the extinction of many of the earth's species.

Forgive us, Lord.

We have not truly appreciated the interdependence of our relationship with creation. We have not recognized the importance of consuming less and living a simpler life for the sustainability of the planet. We have not been willing to change but, instead, have put our hope and trust in other sources, expecting them to save us.

Forgive us, Lord.

We have taken for granted many of the issues related to finding solutions to these problems. We have placed our trust in government, business, and the fields of science and technology—abandoning our responsibility to speak up and take action.

Forgive us, Lord.

Part 2: Commitment

Lord, thank you for your mercy and grace. Thank you for the opportunity to start fresh. From this day forward, we commit to be caretakers—people who take care in actively demonstrating love for the earth and all its creatures.

Help us to be caretakers, Lord.

We commit to get involved, rather than to be indifferent and apathetic.

Help us to be caretakers, Lord.

We commit to the changes that are necessary to reflect your own care and concern for all the world—for all people, all creatures, and all living things.

Help us to be caretakers, Lord.

We commit to be responsible in the way that we live our lives each and every day, acknowledging that the habits we practice not only shape the environment in which we live but also affect future generations.

Help us to be caretakers, Lord.

Amen.

---

[1] Ellen Davis, *Scripture, Culture, and Agriculture* (New York: Cambridge University Press, 2009), 55.

[2] Rueben Job, *Three Simple Rules* (Nashville: Abingdon Press, 2007).

[3] John Wesley's words were "attending upon all the ordinances of God." See *The Book of Discipline* (Nashville: The United Methodist Publishing House, 2008), 74.

2

SESSION TWO:
Consider the Earth

Welcome / Opening Prayer (5 mins.)

Creator God, you made a beautiful home for us, and we have been irresponsible in caring for it. We have caused great damage, and we are saddened and grieved—not only by our destructive actions, but also by our lack of reverence and awe for you and your magnificent creation. God, we acknowledge that this is a spiritual crisis of great proportions. Help us to recapture a sense of mystery and wonder. Help us to consider the lilies and the ravens, remembering that we are your beloved children and that you love and care for us deeply. May we strive less for material things and more for a deeper meaning of life with you, with other human beings, and with creation itself. Amen.

Creation Crisis Question (5 mins.)

Ask: Do you believe that our interest in the planet and the rest of life should be equal to our interest in ourselves? Why or why not?

Allow participants to offer brief responses.

Scripture (5 mins.)

[Jesus] said to his disciples, "Therefore I tell you, do not worry about your life, what you will eat, or about your body, what you will wear. For life is more than food, and the body

*more than clothing. Consider the ravens: they neither sow
nor reap, they have neither storehouse nor barn, and yet God
feeds them. Of how much more value are you than the birds!
And can any of you by worrying add a single hour to your
span of life? If then you are not able to do so small a thing
as that, why do you worry about the rest? Consider the lilies,
how they grow: they neither toil nor spin; yet I tell you, even
Solomon in all his glory was not clothed like one of these.
But if God so clothes the grass of the field, which is alive
today and tomorrow is thrown into the oven, how much more
will he clothe you—you of little faith! And do not keep striving for what you are to eat and what you are to drink, and do
not keep worrying. For it is the nations of the world that
strive after all these things, and your Father knows that you
need them. Instead, strive for his kingdom, and these things
will be given to you as well. . . . For where your treasure is,
there your heart will be also." (Luke 12:22-31, 34)*

Read the Scripture aloud and pause briefly. Read the Scripture
a second time, instructing participants to listen for a word or phrase
that resonates in their spirit. Invite participants to spend a moment
in silent meditation as they consider what God is saying to them
through the Scripture.

Connecting the Dots (40–45 mins.)

Note: More material is provided than you will have time to cover
in one session. In advance, select the leader cues and discussion
questions you want to include, and put a checkmark beside them.

1 We are destroying the home God has given us.

Leader Cue

Read aloud or retell the modern parable about the son who
lived in his father's house (pp. 41–43, *A Hopeful Earth*). Then read
aloud the following, or communicate the points in your own words.

- The origin of the word ecology is from the Greek *oikos*, and it means house. This planet is our house, the home we have to live on. We affect it, and it affects us. Homes require constant upkeep and care. Homes hold significant meaning. Homes are where we cook and eat our food, raise our children, form our memories, and carry out our lives. Home is where the heart is, but that is where the analogy breaks down.

- We are destroying every aspect of the home God has given us. Sometimes this is because we want what God's home has to offer us for our livelihood. Sometimes this is for our own pleasure. Sometimes it is out of ignorance. Regardless, the destruction is wide-scale. Our choices and actions are destroying everything in this home—from the air we breathe to the water we drink to the way we grow the food we eat to the conditions of the climate.

- To better understand this massive assault on life, one must consider HIPPO. HIPPO stands for Habitat destruction, Invasive species, Pollution, (over)Population, and Overconsumption (or overuse) of resources. Each of these five factors contributes to the enormous loss of species we face today.

- What we have done to creation is a disaster. God's home has been spoiled and rendered uninhabitable in many places, affecting its beauty, peoples' livelihood, and its future ability to house many species, including humanity.

Discussion Questions
- What HIPPO components are at work in the ecosystem/environment in which you live? What are some of the concerns regarding habitat destruction, invasive species, pollution, (over)population, and overconsumption/overuse of resources?
- Considering the damage that we have done to the home that God has given us, how do you feel when facing God, the Creator of our home?
- What do we say in our defense?

- In light of the fact that we have trashed God's earth, what does it mean for us to be followers of Jesus? In other words, what should our response be?

2 When we're disconnected from nature, we're increasingly disconnected from God, others, and a respect and reverence for God's house.

Leader Cue

Read aloud the following, or communicate the points in your own words.

- Today we are increasingly separated or disconnected from nature, both physically and spiritually. When this happens, we lose our capacity for wonder and our respect and reverence for God's creation. We fail to see creation's beauty or fragility, and the result is disastrous.
- Abraham Joshua Heschel emphasized throughout his writings that awe precedes faith. When our sense of awe and wonder diminishes, we begin to make ourselves the center of the universe instead of God—which is the very definition of sin. When we're the center of our universe—humanity's sense that nothing or no one exists beyond us—then we lose respect and reverence for God, for others, and for the earth itself.

Discussion Questions
- In what ways are we separated from nature today? How does this affect us?
- What tends to disconnect you from God's creation?
- What can help us to cultivate a sense of wonder for creation?
- How can learning more about science help to increase our awe for the mystery and wonder of God and God's creation?

3 We must consider creation if we want to follow Jesus.

Leader Cue

Read aloud Luke 12:22-31, 34. Then read aloud the following, or communicate the points in your own words.

- Jesus directed his disciples' attention to creation in order to teach them how to live as his followers. He told them to consider the ravens and the lilies—in other words, to ponder and wonder at creation so that they might reorder their lives and values according to what is important. He knew that how we live is connected to the way in which we see creation around us. When we are disconnected with nature, we focus on ourselves and wind up grasping and clinging for material things instead of the spiritual. The result is pride, greed, discontent, dis-ease, and disruption of the created order.

- Jesus' perspective on healthy spiritual living was connected to his agrarian worldview, which was evidenced in his agricultural stories and teachings, such as the planting of seeds (Mark 4:1-20) and talking about the seasons. An agrarian worldview is more than being connected to the soil and farming; it's a system of values and a culture of community, sustainability in all resources, including human resources, and a preservation of what is provided through creation so that it lasts for the next generation.

- Jesus' agrarian worldview influenced his own way of instructing his followers on how to understand their identity, find their sense of importance, and determine how to live in relation to others and God—for their present generation as well as for generations to come. He demonstrated in his teaching that life is more than the material—what we can get out of it for ourselves.

Discussion Questions
- In what ways have we substituted consumerism for faith in our society?

- Considering the lifestyle habits of the average American, what would you say are the priorities of most people today?
- Why do you think we tend to give more emphasis and importance to food and clothing than we should?
- What are some of the connections that Jesus made in his teachings between creation/nature and habits of healthy spiritual living?

4 Jesus reminds us that we are beloved children of God, not consumers.

Leader Cue

Read aloud the following, or communicate the points in your own words.

- The original sin of Adam and Eve was consuming what wasn't theirs to consume. As a result of this disobedience to God, they were thrown out of the garden, and life became much more difficult. They forgot who they were—beloved children of God—and assumed the identity of consumers.
- Just as the Israelites repeatedly chose to worship fertility gods, who promised prosperity and success, today we choose to worship the gods of success, affluence, and materialism. This has impacted our American culture in ways that cause overconsumption and living beyond our means. The results are the depletion of resources, an unsustainable economy, the continued reliance upon fossil fuel, and the pollution of natural resources through waste and disposal. The earth is wasting away as our false identity as consumers leads us to worship prosperity at the expense of others and the earth's resources.
- Jesus reminds us that God cares for the birds and lilies in the field, but more than that, God cares for us. We are the beloved children of God. When we remember who we are,

we become more Christ-like, more holy, and more just. Therefore, we're better able to act out of our beloved selves and love God and our neighbor. Knowing we are not consumers but beloved children of God enables us to worry and strive less.

- Jesus reminds us that life is more than food and clothing—the material things of life. It's about the abundance and the goodness of life that God alone gives us: our lives, our health, our families and relationships of all kinds, this earth, our church, our community. We must remember what we do have and limit our use of what God has given to us so that all may enjoy the goodness of God's creation.

Discussion Questions
- Did you ever think of the original sin of Adam and Eve as being an act of consuming what wasn't theirs to consume? How are we guilty of this sin today?
- What do most people strive for today? Why does striving place us in conflict with others? With the earth?
- What are we meant to strive for, and what happens when we do?
- What would it mean for you to live out of your identity as a beloved child of God, rather than as a consumer? What changes might this bring in your lifestyle?

5 Discouraging messages can keep us from hopeful actions that bring change. The truth is that we can make a real difference in the face of seemingly insurmountable problems in our world today.

Leader Cue
Read aloud the following, or communicate the points in your own words.

- The world tells us that we can't make a difference; we can't solve the problems of our communities, state, nation, and world. The mantra of what we can't do lies within us; and so we give up, despair, and grow cynical. There's much to discourage us, and the world's messages—sometimes even the church's unintended messages—can keep us from the hopeful actions that bring change.

- Jesus reminds us not to worry. God who is able to create the birds of the air and the lilies of the field is able to do amazing and wonderful things in and through creation. That same God is able to empower us to do what seems impossible: to feed the hungry, heal the sick, and live each day with hope and joy even as we face life's adversity and challenges.
- Jesus' message empowers us through hope, enabling us to make the changes in our own lives and in the world around us that are necessary to be better stewards of the earth.

Discussion Questions
- What discourages you regarding your ability to make a difference in caring for the earth?
- How do the teachings of Jesus empower us related to our ability to work toward a hopeful future?
- How can we work together to make a difference in the face of the seemingly insurmountable problems in our world today?

Expanding Our Horizons (15 mins. – 90-minute session only)

In Jesus' day, most people in Israel lived by farming. Their family and community lives were governed by the cycles of sowing and harvesting various crops. Plan to gather additional information related to this agrarian lifestyle of Jesus' day. In advance of the session, assign one or more persons specific topics to research on the Internet or at a public or church library, such as farming/shepherding and everyday life in Jesus' day. Invite them to share their findings with the group.

Continuing the Journey (5 mins.)

In session 1 we learned of John Wesley's three simple rules. The second simple rule is: Do good. Wesley described "doing good" as "being in every kind merciful after their power; as they have opportunity, doing good of every possible sort, and, as far as possible, to all. . . ."[1] Learning to do good is being mindful of how our lifestyle, habits, and practices affect the lives of others and being merciful as we "have opportunity."

A Commitment for Individuals:
- What are some ways that you can be more proactive in caring for the earth?
- Make a list of small ways you can personally make a difference and try one of them this week.
- Also, make a conscious effort to be more observant of God's creation whenever you are outdoors this week.

A Commitment for Groups: Identify one seemingly insurmountable problem related to the care of the environment and brainstorm ways you can work together as a group to begin making a positive difference. Choose one of these ideas and write a plan of action. Then set a date for when you will take your first step together.

Wonder and Worship (10 mins. – 90-minute session only)

Weather permitting, go outside and find a quiet, peaceful place where you can sit and observe the beauty of God's creation as a group. Or take a walk outdoors together. Invite participants to meditate and pray silently while sitting or walking. After several minutes, offer a closing prayer expressing awe, wonder, and thanksgiving for all of God's creation.

In case of inclement weather, remain indoors and invite participants to close their eyes and imagine themselves in a quiet, serene, and beautiful outdoor setting of their choosing. Give verbal cues such as, "Feel the wind blowing . . . ," "Listen to the sounds of nature all around you . . . ," and "Observe the living things that are stirring near or far . . . ," pausing sufficiently between each cue. Invite participants to offer silent prayers throughout this time of guided meditation. In closing, say aloud a prayer expressing awe, wonder, and thanksgiving for all of God's creation.

---

[1] *Book of Discipline*, 2008, p. 73.

3

SESSION THREE:
The Love of Stuff

Welcome / Opening Prayer (5 mins.)

Lord Jesus, you talked about money and wealth more than you did about heaven and eternal life. This tells us there is some connection between money and heaven—between wealth and eternal life. We're no different than the man in the parable you told who wanted to build bigger barns. We yearn and strive for more, bigger, and better stuff. We are self-centered, selfish, and greedy. We want what we want when we want it, and we feel entitled to it. We have allowed our love of stuff to separate us from others and from you. We have trusted in material things rather than in you. Forgive us, Lord. Help us to recognize that our greed causes us to accumulate more than we need at the expense of others—our neighbors near and far. May we connect our overconsumption with others' lack of basics, and may we be filled with remorse and compassion, leading to repentance and lasting change—for the good of ourselves, others, and all creation. Amen.

Creation Crisis Question (5 mins.)

Ask: How does greed affect ecology/the environment? What is the relationship between stuff and sustainable living?

Allow participants to offer brief responses.

Scripture (5 mins.)

> *Someone in the crowd said to [Jesus], "Teacher, tell my brother to divide the family inheritance with me." But he said to him, "Friend, who set me to be a judge or arbitrator over you?" And he said to them, "Take care! Be on your guard against all kinds of greed; for one's life does not consist in the abundance of possessions." Then he told them a parable: "The land of a rich man produced abundantly. And he thought to himself, 'What should I do, for I have no place to store my crops?' Then he said, 'I will do this: I will pull down my barns and build larger ones, and there I will store all my grain and my goods. And I will say to my soul, Soul, you have ample goods laid up for many years; relax, eat, drink, be merry.' But God said to him, 'You fool! This very night your life is being demanded of you. And the things you have prepared, whose will they be?' So it is with those who store up treasures for themselves but are not rich toward God." (Luke 12:13-21)*

Read the Scripture aloud and pause briefly. Read the Scripture a second time, instructing participants to listen for a word or phrase that resonates in their spirit. Invite participants to spend a moment in silent meditation as they consider what God is saying to them through the Scripture.

Connecting the Dots (30–40 mins.)

Note: For a 90-minute session, you will need to decrease the time for Connecting the Dots to 30 minutes in order to allow for a longer Expanding Our Horizons activity. As usual, more material is provided than you will have time to cover in one session. In advance, select the leader cues and discussion questions you want to include, and put a checkmark beside them.

1 Stuff makes us selfish.

Leader Cue

Read aloud the following, or communicate the points in your own words.

- The economic downturn of 2008 caused many Americans to come face to face with the overconsumption of goods in our lives. The underlying greed, or love of stuff, in our culture was revealed as the economy spun out of control.
- When we strive for money and possessions, we minimize the importance of the relationships in our lives. Acquiring stuff keeps us separated from our literal neighbors as well as our neighbors around the world.
- What makes connecting Jesus and the environment so controversial is that it challenges one of our American core values: individualism. Individualism is in opposition to the ways in which Jesus wants us to live. When we practice more environmentally sound behaviors and make changes to our lifestyle, we rediscover more and more community in our lives.
- Bill McKibben says that "wild individualism" makes us care more about our stuff than our neighbors, near and far, now and in the future, and therefore alienates us not only from our neighbor, but also from God.[1]
- Jesus has a lot to say about our accumulation and reliance upon material wealth, because it impacts how we relate to God. If we place our trust and security in God, we have less need for things that do not last.

Discussion Questions
- In what ways has the economic downturn helped you to recognize "the love of stuff"—within and/or around you?

- As Christians, how can we better give to those we love?
- How does the desire for stuff affect our relationships with our neighbors—those both near and far? How has the pursuit and maintenance of stuff affected the relationships in your own life?
- How is individualism in opposition to the ways Jesus wants us to live? How does it alienate us from others and from God?
- How do environmentally sound practices help to build community?
- What is the relationship between trust in God and desire for material things? How easy or difficult is it for you to let go of stuff? What do you believe this reveals about your relationship with God?

2 Our stuff tells our story.

Leader Cue

Read aloud the following, or communicate the points in your own words.

- If we want to truly understand ourselves, we must truly understand our stuff. This requires asking questions such as, What is stuff made of? Who makes our stuff and where? How do we get stuff? How do we choose what stuff we need? Where does our stuff we no longer want or need go? Does it just go "away"?
- In the brilliant and informative short, free, downloadable film, *The Story of Stuff*, Annie Leonard explains the process of stuff: the steps of extraction, production, distribution, consumption, and disposal.[2] Examination of these steps gives us the information to understand our stuff and thus ourselves.
- The extraction process, the first step in creating stuff, hurts the poor, hurts the third world, and hurts the planet. Likewise,

<u>production</u> of stuff hurts the poor, takes advantage of the third world, and pollutes the planet. In <u>distribution</u>, the resources to make stuff and the stuff itself move all around the globe. The final step in the process is selling stuff, or <u>consumption</u>. Planned obsolescence contributes to our consumption, resulting in a <u>disposal</u> problem. The structure of our consumptive society harms the poor of this world (domestic and foreign), destroys ecosystems including all the life within them, pollutes air, water, and land, and uses valuable resources.

- Jesus' teachings question why we want more, bigger, and better. We have to have some stuff in order to live, but we need to limit our stuff. More, better, bigger isn't healthy for our hearts because it crowds out our love for our neighbors and the environment.

Discussion Questions
- How does understanding our stuff help us to understand ourselves?
- Think of your favorite "thing." What story or process might be behind it? Discuss the steps of extraction, production, distribution, consumption, and disposal as they relate to several material things.
- What drives our desire for more, bigger, and better? Why do you think we struggle with limiting the amount of stuff we have? What is one area where you find it difficult to eliminate or limit "stuff"?
- Why is striving after and accumulating stuff unhealthy for our hearts?

Expanding Our Horizons (30 mins. – 90-minute session only)

Make arrangements to watch the free, downloadable film, *The Story of Stuff*, as a group (www.storyofstuff.org, allow 20 mins.). Then have a 10-minute group discussion, selecting from the following questions:

- What stuff of yours did you think of first while watching the video?
- What feelings did the video evoke?
- What are two things you learned from the video?
- Who is all the "stuff" for, and who pays for all the "stuff"?
- What drives this stuff system?
- Is there anything you have learned from the video that is in conflict with your faith?
- What are things we as individuals, the church, and the greater community do to change our stuff and the system of our stuff?

Continuing the Journey (5 mins.)

John Wesley's third simple rule is to stay in love with God through means of keeping up spiritual practices, or "ordinances." Caring for the earth can be considered a way of staying in love with God because it includes practices that "bind us to God every day but . . . also . . . heal the pain, injustice, and inequality of our world."[3]

A Commitment for Individuals:
- Focus on loving God and others more than your possessions.
- Work on your attentiveness to appreciating what you *have* rather than what you *lack*.
- Identify some unnecessary stuff in your life that you might sell or give away.

A Commitment for Groups: Inextricably linked with staying in love with God is loving our neighbors—near and far, rich and poor. Encourage participants to get rid of some of the "stuff" in their lives. Plan and hold a rummage sale together, giving the proceeds to neighbors in need within your community and around the globe.

Wonder and Worship (10 mins. – 90-minute session only)

Light a candle and place a visual symbol representing "treasure" before the group (e.g., a treasure chest).

Read aloud the following:

Do you have a desire for more, bigger, or better stuff? Are you willing to buy now and pay later so that you can have what you want? These are signs of the basic greed within us as human beings. Greed has been compared to a virus that takes over like an infection. It multiplies and increases within us, making us want every new thing we see and causing us to feel deprived when we can't have it.

Jesus told us we are to be rich toward God. He also said, "Store up for yourselves treasures in heaven, where neither moth nor rust consumes and where thieves do not break in and steal" (Matthew 6:20).

Give each participant two index cards and a pen or pencil. On one card, have them write some material desire that God is calling them to relinquish. On the other card, have them write a spiritual treasure—a way they are rich toward God. Instruct participants to take the cards home with them and put them in a place where they will see them regularly, reminding them to seek heavenly rather than earthly treasures. Close with a prayer.

---

[1] Bill McKibben, "Hot and Bothered: Facing Up to Global Warming," *Christian Century*, July 11, 2006, 29, 31.

[2] *The Story of Stuff*, film by Annie Leonard (Free Range Studios, 2007), http://www.storyofstuff.org.

[3] Job, 58.

4

SESSION FOUR:
Creating Hell All Around Us

Welcome / Opening Prayer (5 mins.)

Creator God, in your perfection and wisdom you made everything in the world in such a way that all by-products and unused materials and remains are used by something else. Everything in nature is recycled. In fact, apart from human beings, pollution would not even exist! Unfortunately, pollution is all too real. We all know that pollution is a problem, and yet it's easy to adopt an "out of sight, out of mind" attitude. We forget that even though we may not be able to see it once we get rid of it, the waste that we dispose of still affects the planet—and the people who live on it—in dramatic and significant ways. Help us to understand that our overproduction of waste creates "hell on earth" for many of the world's helpless poor who actually have to live amidst the refuse. Open our eyes to the everyday ways we are contributing to the problem, and make us willing to make the changes that are necessary to make a positive difference. Amen.

Creation Crisis Question (5 mins.)

Ask: How does our garbage affect the poor of this world? Allow participants to offer brief responses.

Scripture (5 mins.)

"There was a rich man who was dressed in purple and fine linen and who feasted sumptuously every day. And at his gate lay a poor man named Lazarus, covered with sores, who longed to satisfy his hunger with what fell from the rich man's table; even the dogs would come and lick his sores. The poor man died and was carried away by the angels to be with Abraham. The rich man also died and was buried. In Hades, where he was being tormented, he looked up and saw Abraham far away with Lazarus by his side. He called out, 'Father Abraham, have mercy on me, and send Lazarus to dip the tip of his finger in water and cool my tongue; for I am in agony in these flames.' But Abraham said, 'Child, remember that during your lifetime you received your good things, and Lazarus in like manner evil things; but now he is comforted here, and you are in agony. Besides all this, between you and us a great chasm has been fixed, so that those who might want to pass from here to you cannot do so, and no one can cross from there to us.' He said, 'Then, father, I beg you to send him to my father's house—for I have five brothers—that he may warn them, so that they will not also come into this place of torment.' Abraham replied, 'They have Moses and the prophets; they should listen to them.' He said, 'No, father Abraham; but if someone goes to them from the dead, they will repent.' He said to him, 'If they do not listen to Moses and the prophets, neither will they be convinced even if someone rises from the dead.'" (Luke 16:19-31)

Read the Scripture aloud and pause briefly. Read the Scripture a second time, instructing participants to listen for a word or phrase that resonates in their spirit. Invite participants to spend a moment in silent meditation as they consider what God is saying to them through the Scripture.

Connecting the Dots (40–45 mins.)

Note: More material is provided than you will have time to cover in one session. In advance, select the leader cues and discussion questions you want to include, and put a checkmark beside them.

1 Our lifestyle of throw-away living creates hells on this planet, affecting the land and many of its people.

Leader Cue

Read aloud the following, or communicate the points in your own words.

- Waste doesn't occur in nature. In nature, all of the by-products, unused materials, and remains are the requirements of something else. Everything in nature is recycled. In the absence of humans, no piles of toxicity or garbage would exist.
- Pollution—which can be roughly grouped into land, air, and water pollution—is changing the planet in disturbing and significant ways.
- The United States, with only 4.6 percent of the world's population, creates one third of its solid waste. Each American produces 4.5 pounds of garbage per day. The vast majority of this is sent to one of our over 10,000 landfills.
- Limiting and recycling what we use is helpful, but it doesn't address the heart of the issue of our consumption and throwaway lifestyle, and it fails to truly lift the veil between what we do and the hellish consequences of our actions.
- Landfills are, in a sense, chemical time bombs as their lifespan is around forty or fifty years.
- The profit in garbage is the main reason we do less recycling than we could.
- Often what waste is not legal, too dangerous, or too expensive to dispose of safely or recycle is dumped on other people—poor countries, poor people, and children.

Discussion Questions
- Have you ever considered the fact that without human beings there would be no pollution? How does this make you feel?
- Discuss some of the ways that pollution is changing and disturbing the planet. Which of these changes disturbs you most, and why?

- What does the fact that the United States has 4.6 percent of the world's population but creates ones third of the world's solid waste say about our culture, our character, and our values?
- What are some of the hellish consequences of our over-consumption and overproduction of waste?
- Why is recycling an insufficient answer to the problem?

2 Pollution has devastating effects.

Leader Cue

Read aloud the following, or communicate the points in your own words.

- All forms of waste disposal and pollution are impacting our environment, affecting first the poor of the world but quickly the wealthy of the world, too.
- Pollution has health, economic, political, and many other affects.
- Pollution creates environmental refugees.
- We bridge a bit of the chasm between the wealthy and poor when we participate in providing ministries of mercy. But mercy is not enough. We also need to provide justice ministries to prevent the chasms that exist between us and those who live in such squalor.

Discussion Questions
- Why is waste disposal such a critical issue for all people—both poor and wealthy?
- Discuss the various effects of pollution on health, economics, politics, and religion.
- What are environmental refugees? How are they created?
- Why are ministries of mercy not enough to prevent the chasm that exists between the poor and the wealthy? What are justice ministries, and why are they essential?

- What can we do to help those who live in "garbage dump" environments? Which of your ideas are acts of mercy and which are acts of justice?

Expanding Our Horizons (15 mins. – 90-minute session only)

There are three major categories of pollution: land, air, and water. Within these categories are multiple subcategories, such as e-waste and medical waste. In advance of the session, assign one or more persons one category or subcategory to research, and have them to share their findings with the group, providing statistics and details specific to your region or area, if possible.

Or, have someone investigate various justice ministries to the marginalized in developing nations, providing a summary of each ministry to the group.

Continuing the Journey (5 mins.)

Doing no harm, according to Wesley, included economic and social justice actions such as avoiding slaveholding and borrowing without the likelihood of paying. Doing no harm is a way of looking at any decision we make in terms of "if I do this, or more likely don't do this, eat this, drink this, throw this away, then will I have prevented harm to the earth and the people who live upon it?"

A Commitment for Individuals:
- Consider the ways we as individuals, organizations, and countries do harm to developing nations and to the helpless poor.
- Make a commitment to begin reducing your waste production. Go beyond recycling and consider how you can prevent unnecessary waste or garbage in your life. Some ideas to consider include buying fresh produce instead of canned vegetables, buying multi-purpose products, keeping disposable goods to a minimum and using more permanent products, finding creative ways to reuse items, etc.
- Search the Internet for other ideas, and select 2-3 to try.

A Commitment for Groups:

Option 1: What can your group/church do—or stop doing—to prevent harm to the earth and the people who live upon it? Identify one action and follow through. Consider initiating a church-wide awareness campaign.

Option 2: Investigate various justice ministries to the poor and marginalized in developing nations (see Expanding Our Horizons) and choose one ministry to support—both financially and, if possible, actively.

Wonder and Worship (10 mins. – 90-minute session only)

In advance of the session, purchase 4 large poster boards. Write the following words on each poster—one word on one side and the other word on the other side:

Indifferent/ Compassionate
Self-centered / Self-sacrificing
Lazy / Involved
Greedy / Generous

Invite four participants to come forward and hold the posters, showing the negative words to the group. As they stand before the group, read aloud the first part of the following prayer. Then, as you begin the second part of the prayer, have the participants flip the posters over one at a time as each positive word is spoken aloud.

Part 1:

God of all creation, we have been indifferent to the harmful effects of our excessive, waste-producing lifestyles—not only to the planet, but also to the marginalized poor.

We have been self-centered, caring more about our wants and desires than about the needs of those who struggle to survive day to day.

We have been lazy, unwilling to give up our conveniences and to take steps to make a difference.

And we have been greedy, caring more about budgets and bottom lines than about choices and changes that allow others to live a better quality of life.

<u>Part 2:</u>
Wake us up from our indifference, Lord! Open our eyes! We long to be like your Son, Jesus, who was . . .

Compassionate . . .
Self-sacrificing . . .
Involved (in meeting the needs of the poor and helpless) . . .
Generous

Today we express our desire to become more and more like Jesus. Today we commit ourselves to doing good rather than harm to the helpless poor of the world. Today we choose to make practical lifestyle changes in order to reduce the pollution in our world for the good of all, especially those who are suffering and struggling to survive. In Jesus' name we pray. Amen.

5

SESSION FIVE:
Take It to the Water

Welcome / Opening Prayer (5 mins.)

Lord, most of us take fresh, clean, available water for granted. But that's not the case around the world. Even in some parts of the United States, water is a scarce resource. Wherever water isn't available, there is conflict and poverty. Water means life or death, peace or war. Water is precious. Water is life. Open our eyes to recognize the immense value of clean, safe water. May we never take it for granted again. And may we be moved to compassion and action on behalf of those who do not have access to it. In the name of Jesus, our Living Water, we pray. Amen.

Creation Crisis Question (5 mins.)

Ask: Is water a human right or a marketable commodity? Allow participants to offer brief responses.

Scripture (5 mins.)

[Jesus] left Judea and started back to Galilee. But he had to go through Samaria. So he came to a Samaritan city called Sychar. . . . A Samaritan woman came to draw water, and Jesus said to her, "Give me a drink." (His disciples had gone to the city to buy food.) The Samaritan woman said to

him, "How is it that you, a Jew, ask a drink of me, a woman of Samaria?" (Jews do not share things in common with Samaritans.) Jesus answered her, "If you knew the gift of God, and who it is that is saying to you, 'Give me a drink,' you would have asked him, and he would have given you living water." The woman said to him, "Sir, you have no bucket, and the well is deep. Where do you get that living water? Are you greater than our ancestor Jacob, who gave us the well, and with his sons and his flocks drank from it?" Jesus said to her, "Everyone who drinks of this water will be thirsty again, but those who drink of the water that I will give them will never be thirsty. The water that I will give will become in them a spring of water gushing up to eternal life." The woman said to him, "Sir, give me this water, so that I may never be thirsty or have to keep coming here to draw water." ... The woman said to him, "I know that Messiah is coming" (who is called Christ). "When he comes, he will proclaim all things to us." Jesus said to her, "I am he, the one who is speaking to you." ... Then the woman left her water jar and went back to the city. She said to the people, "Come and see a man who told me everything I have ever done! He cannot be the Messiah, can he?" They left the city and were on their way to him. (John 4:3-5a, 7-15, 25-26, 28-30)

Read the Scripture aloud and pause briefly. Read the Scripture a second time, instructing participants to listen for a word or phrase that resonates in their spirit. Invite participants to spend a moment in silent meditation as they consider what God is saying to them through the Scripture.

Connecting the Dots (40–45 mins.)

Note: More material is provided than you will have time to cover in one session. In advance, select the leader cues and discussion questions you want to include, and put a checkmark beside them.

1 Water is an issue of poverty.

Leader Cue

Read aloud the following, or communicate the points in your own words.

- Water is an issue of life and death. All life requires water. Humans can survive for only a few days without water. Thus, water becomes an issue of health, economics, politics, and government.
- Water is an issue of the poor and a major key in ending poverty.
- Because water is essential in maintaining the balance of the ecosystem upon which we depend for so many goods and services, it is absolutely essential that we face head-on the issues of water quality, distribution, access, sustainable use, and rights.
- While we realize that we use water to shower, wash dishes, flush the toilet, and water the garden, we may not realize that many of our other activities also require water.
- There is currently enough freshwater on earth to sustain life, but the water is not distributed equally or, more important, according to human need.
- There is an inherent conflict of interest between the needs of poor nations and private water companies. Often people cannot afford the new, clean, privatized water that is available, and so they chose to return to the streams of free water that contain waterborne diseases, such as cholera.[1]

Discussion Questions
- How is water an issue of poverty? How does it contribute to poverty, and how can it help to end poverty?
- As Christians living in a society where clean water is readily available, why should we be concerned about issues of water quality, distribution, access, sustainable use, and rights?

- What are the ways you use and rely upon water every day? Think beyond the usual activities of consumption, personal hygiene, and food preparation.
- Do you think our use of water should be unlimited? Why or why not? What water is ours to use?
- Do you think the location that we return the water to, or the condition we return the water in, matters? Why or why not?
- Do you think that countries own the water that flows through them, and do they have the right to use the water as they see fit? Why or why not?
- What can we do to help ensure the equal distribution of water? What are possible solutions to the unequal distribution of water?

2 Water is an issue of peace.

Leader Cue

Read aloud the following, or communicate the points in your own words.

- Wherever water isn't available, there is conflict—conflicts over quantity, management, and sustainable use of water create rivals.
- While we associate war with differences based on religion and politics, war based on sharing a scarce resource such as water is real. It is said that if the twentieth century brought oil wars, the twenty-first century will bring water wars.
- We go to war for oil, and we think we need oil. Water will be the next resource scarcity but with a greater price because there are no alternatives to water.
- Issues of quality, accessibility, and cost of water create conflict around water rights. Is water a commodity that can be sold? Who should own and manage water is a complicated

question. Typically, governments own water and manage it as a public resource. However, it is becoming increasingly more frequent that cities and even nations are turning over their water to private companies to be managed. With private management comes private ownership.

Discussion Questions
- How is water an issue of peace? How does water create conflict and rivals?
- How might we work to prevent wars based on sharing a scare resource such as water?
- Do you believe water is a right or a marketable commodity that can/should be sold? Why?
- If you belicvc that water is a right, who pays for it?
- If you believe that water is a marketable commodity, how can we ensure access to water for the poor?
- What are possible solutions to water rivalries in our world?
- What do you think Jesus' response to our water crisis and its affect on peace, poverty, and the planet would be?

3 Bottled water is not good stewardship.

Leader Cue
Read aloud the following, or communicate the points in your own words.

- Plastic bottles have a big carbon footprint. It requires a lot of energy and water to process and ship bottled water, and the bottles are a major pollution problem when it comes to their disposal.[2]
- Although water bottles are recyclable, we recycle less than 25 percent of them and the rest are pitched into landfills at the rate of 38 billion water bottles a year or $1 billion worth of plastic.[3]

- Bottled water for Americans is simply a convenience that consumes more resources than is justifiable in most situations. It's consumerism at its worst.

Discussion Questions
- What have you learned about bottled water that you did not know previously?
- In what ways is bottled water poor stewardship?
- Do you agree that bottled water is consumerism at its worst? Why or why not?

Expanding Our Horizons (15 mins. – 90-minute session only)
In advance of the session, have one person to research areas of the world where clean, safe, available water is a scarcity. Have another to research clean water initiatives through organizations such as United Methodist Committee on Relief (UMCOR.org), Blood:Water Mission (http://www.bloodwatermission.com), or Ginghamsburg Church's Miracle Offering (www.theSudanProject.org). Allow them to share their findings with the group.

Continuing the Journey (5 mins.)
When Jesus spoke to the woman at the well, he asked her for a drink, and in return, he gave her living water. Our neighbors are dying of thirst, and our consumption practices are in need of improvement. Together we must learn to do good by paying attention to our baptism call to "sit at the wells of life" with our brothers and sisters.

A Commitment for Individuals:
- Think about the water you consume each week.
- Remember your baptism; honor and enjoy the availability of clean water.
- Find a way to participate in providing clean water, either through your habits or by joining with others to be part of clean water initiatives (see Expanding Our Horizons).

A Commitment for Groups: One pastor challenged his congregation to put aside one dollar every time they drank bottled water. If they were given or asked for a glass of water in a restaurant and didn't drink it, they were to put aside one dollar. They collected the money and used it to purchase a well in Africa. It was a way for them to become more mindful of our misuse of the water that we consume at a high expense to ourselves and at the expense of others. Make a commitment as a group to adopt this practice for six to twelve months, collecting the money and contributing it for the purchase of a well in a place where clean, safe water is scarce. You also might consider challenging the entire congregation to join you in this effort.

Wonder and Worship (10 mins. – 90-minute session only)

The story of the woman at the well reminds us that as followers of Jesus, we have received the life-giving waters of baptism. Remember your baptism together by reaffirming the covenant made at your baptism. Use the "Congregational Reaffirmation of the Baptismal Covenant" (*The United Methodist Hymnal*, pp. 50–52) or some similar service of reaffirmation. If any members of the group have not received baptism and would like to do so, baptize them prior to the reaffirmation of faith (see the section "Baptism" on p. 47 of *The United Methodist Hymnal*).

---

[1] *Blue Gold: World Water Wars*, film by Sam Bozzo (Purple Turtle Films, 2010).
[2] "Message in a Bottle," by Charles Fishman, *Fast Company*, http://www.fast company.com/magazine/117/features-message-in-a-bottle.html, p. 7.
[3] Ibid.

6

SESSION SIX:
Bless This Food!

Welcome / Opening Prayer (5 mins.)

God, you have graciously and bountifully provided food for all living things, yet so many people in the world simply do not have enough to eat. It's not because we are unable to produce enough food for everyone on the planet. The problem is largely due to our industrialized food system and the rules that govern it. Though it often seems that the problem of world hunger is simply too big and daunting, remind us today that solutions begin when one or two individuals work together. Motivate us to get involved, not only in policy making but also in habit breaking. Show us that even simple changes in the ways that we shop and eat can help to ensure that the food on all our tables, as well as the food we share with our neighbors throughout the world, is blessed, holy, and healthy for those who eat it as well as those who produce it. Encourage us to begin taking small steps and to continually ask ourselves where we are and what our next steps should be. In Jesus' name. Amen.

Creation Crisis Question (5 mins.)

Ask: Why do you think we have moved away from a process of being in connection and partnership with the planet to one of mass-producing as much food as possible with minimal regard for the planet?

Allow participants to offer brief responses.

Scripture (5 mins.)

> *The day was drawing to a close, and the twelve came to him and said, "Send the crowd away, so that they may go into the surrounding villages and countryside, to lodge and get provisions; for we are here in a deserted place." But he said to them, "You give them something to eat." They said, "We have no more than five loaves and two fish—unless we are to go and buy food for all these people." For there were about five thousand men. And he said to his disciples, "Make them sit down in groups of about fifty each." They did so and made them all sit down. And taking the five loaves and the two fish, he looked up to heaven, and blessed and broke them, and gave them to the disciples to set before the crowd. And all ate and were filled. What was left over was gathered up, twelve baskets of broken pieces. (Luke 9:12-17)*

Read the Scripture aloud and pause briefly. Read the Scripture a second time, instructing participants to listen for a word or phrase that resonates in their spirit. Invite participants to spend a moment in silent meditation as they consider what God is saying to them through the Scripture.

Connecting the Dots (40–45 mins.)

Note: More material is provided than you will have time to cover in one session. In advance, select the leader cues and discussion questions you want to include, and put a checkmark beside them.

1 We are to be people who care about feeding our neighbors.

Leader Cue

Read aloud the following, or communicate the points in your own words.

- Often we think global issues like hunger are unsolvable because we're overwhelmed by them, but solutions begin with one or two people working together for the common good, changing habits, asking different questions, and doing new things.
- Our food cannot be blessed if it has arrived on our table—or if we eat it—in a fashion that brings injustice, bloodshed, disease, poverty, violence, or warfare to others.
- Jesus calls us to see one another with love and respect, making sure that all our tables and the food we share with one another is blessed, holy, and healthy for those who produce it as well as those who eat it.
- We are to be people who care about the ways in which others are exploited in the production of our food.
- We are to be people who care that there's not enough food for others and that food scarcity causes violence in our world.
- When Jesus said, "Do this in memory of me," he meant that we are to repeat the patterns of sharing in God's economy with our neighbors. Jesus expects us to share the food we have with others.

Discussion Questions
- What does it mean to say that our food cannot be blessed if it has arrived on our table—or if it we eat it—in a way that brings injustice, bloodshed, disease, poverty, violence, or warfare to others?
- What steps can we take to make sure that our food is blessed, holy, and healthy for those who produce it as well as those who eat it?
- What are some ways in which other people are exploited in the production of our food? Why should we care about this?
- What are some practical ways we can share the food we have with others?

2 The system that produces our food is filled with injustices and unethical practices.

Leader Cue

Read aloud the following, or communicate the points in your own words.

- Many of the farmers who produce our food struggle economically.
- Seventy percent of the corn, 80 percent of the soy, and one-third of our marine catch are used to feed factory-farmed or feedlot animals. These animals are raised, transported, and slaughtered using inhumane conditions and practices that breed disease, pollute the air and water, and risk the well-being of humans at various steps of the process.
- The animals we eat produce more than twenty times the waste humans in our country do, but there is no sewage system in place to deal with the waste, allowing it to pollute our waterways.
- The system of food production relies on 2.4 million pounds of pesticides per year in the United States alone, and this figure does not take into account the chemicals added to animal feed, the steroids or antibiotics pumped into animals, and the chemicals added to packaged food in processing.
- The system of our food production uses ten times more energy, in the forms of fossil fuel energy primarily, to produce the food than it provides to the people eating it! In other words, it takes ten units of fossil fuel energy to put one unit of food energy on the table.
- Much of what we eat is so modified, processed, and packaged that it bears little or no resemblance to anything grown or raised or caught in the natural world. The vast majority of the food we eat is produced with processes that cause great harm to our bodies, our planet, and our spirits.
- A change in production of our food that would allow for a more ethical treatment of animals, better environmental use of the planet, and improved health conditions of workers and

consumers would indirectly decrease efficiency and profit—the goals of industrialized food production.

- As a nation and as a world, we are able to produce enough food for everyone on this planet to eat a balanced and nutritious diet. The problem is the system that produces our food, the rules that govern that system, and the money that pays for the system.
- A just society doesn't encourage highly processed foods full of salt, fat, and sugar to be significantly less expensive than healthy food. In a just society, poor families are not forced to choose less healthy foods.
- The current industrialized food system is unjust to farmers, to the poor in this country, to the animals we consume, and to the developing world. The industrialized system's goals to maximize efficiency and profit come at a cost. This cost is paid for by poor people, people who suffer from food-related disease (such as type 2 diabetes), the animals, and the least among us worldwide.

Discussion Questions
- How has food and food production changed since the time of your grandmother?
- What assumptions do you make about where your food comes from? How your food is grown or raised? How it is processed and what is in it?
- In what ways is our food system unjust and unethical? Consider the farmers, the poor in this country, the animals we consume, and the developing world.
- It has been said that in our food system, "animals are not animals, they are food machines." Do you agree? Why or why not?
- What about the process of feedlot and factory-farmed meat production can you not bless?
- What kinds of changes could we make in our food production system in order to benefit our bodies, our spirits, and our planet? What are the challenges to making these changes a reality?

3 "Just eating" is a way to care for the earth, our bodies, and our neighbors.

Leader Cue

Read aloud the following, or communicate the points in your own words.

- "Just eating" involves acts of justice. Policy is difficult to understand and participate in or advocate, but it is the most systemic and transforming action we can take to eliminate poverty and hunger in the United States.
- "Just eating" is eating in such a way that we care for the earth, our bodies, and our neighbors. It's also about expecting that our food is grown in such a way that the earth can continue to sustain life for all and not just for some—both now and in the future, both in the United States and around the world.
- "Just eating" involves adopting "food rules" (guidelines for food production, preparation, and eating) that help us to eat not according to the bathroom scales but according to the scales of justice.

Discussion Questions
- How would you define or explain "just eating"?
- What are some practical ways we can get involved in policy making regarding food production, processing, and distribution?
- What are some specific steps toward "just eating" you can take as an individual? How could a community make changes?
- What would it look like for the greater church to take steps toward more just, ethical food choices?
- Discuss the food rules of Michael Pollan and Sarah Ehrman (see pp. 127 and 129 in *A Hopeful Earth*). How can these rules help us to care for the earth, our bodies, and our neighbors? Which of these rules would you like to adopt for yourself and your family?

- If Jesus were alive today, what do you think he would think of our food? Do you think he could bless the food and the food production process?

Expanding Our Horizons (15 mins. – 90-minute session only)

In advance of the session, have one person research traditional farming (family-owned farms that grow food for the local community or surrounding areas without the use of chemicals and within the larger natural system). Have another person research the industrialized food system (industrialized, corporately controlled farms geared to maximize efficiency and profit). Allow them to present their findings to the group, and compare and contrast the two systems.

Continuing the Journey (5 mins.)

We have ignored, neglected, and outright denied our responsibility to care for the earth in so many ways. Practicing "just eating" is a way to repent of our neglect and begin to care for the earth as well as our neighbors.

A Commitment for Individuals:
- Consider how you can take steps—even small steps—toward healthier, more environmentally sound, and ethical eating.
- Be sure to say grace for the food you enjoy each day this week.

A Commitment for Groups: Consider ways that your group can promote and support eating according to environmentally sound food rules. You might host a farmer's market, share grass-fed beef or other local meats from a local farmer, or cook and eat healthy foods together more regularly.

Wonder and Worship (10 mins. – 90-minute session only)

Share in Holy Communion together, celebrating God's provision of both physical and spiritual nourishment and life. (See pp. 6–16 in *The United Methodist Hymnal.*)